Twenty to

Papercuts

Paper Panda

Search Press

First published in 2015

Search Press Limited
Wellwood, North Farm Road,
Tunbridge Wells, Kent TN2 3DR

Reprinted 2015

Print ISBN: 978-1-78221-191-4
ebook ISBN: 978-1-78126-250-4

Suppliers
If you have difficulty in obtaining any of the
materials and equipment mentioned in this book,
then please visit the Search Press website for
details of suppliers: www.searchpress.com

Printed in China

Dedication

*With many thanks to my hordes of fabulous
Facebook followers, my wonderful team and my family
for believing in me, especially my long-suffering husband,
now affectionately known as Mr P.
You will never again have your own identity.*

Contents

Introduction

Hello! My name is Panda – well, it isn't really, but that is the name I have acquired over the past handful of years along my papercutting journey with my company, Paper Panda.

I am a professional papercutter working in a small Cotswold village called Bourton-on-the-Water. My designs are homely, comforting, happy and generally reflect my life and my quiet country existence.

The templates I have designed have a difficulty rating of 1–5, indicated by the number of scalpels at the top of each project so, if you are a complete beginner, practise with the 1–3 templates first, then progress to the 4s and 5s when you have gained a little experience and confidence. Please do not be disheartened if your papercutting is not perfect straight away – it really does get better with time and practice. Papercutting is a lovely pastime, very relaxing and therapeutic – it is something to be enjoyed, rather than worrying about perfecting your cuts within the first half hour. So take it slowly and have fun with it.

A few of my designs have definite uses, such as the bookmarks and the place cards, but remember that a papercut is a thing of beauty in itself and makes a lovely decoration, whether you frame it or not.

This book may be small, but it is also perfectly formed. Enjoy!

The level of difficulty (1–5) is indicated by the number of scalpel icons.

Tools and materials

All the templates in this book have been designed to be fairly simple, and possible to make with a relatively small number of tools. Those described below are all you should need to accomplish any of the designs included here.

A **scalpel**, made up of a **blade** and **handle**, is the best implement to use for papercutting. **These are surgical grade blades, so please ensure you are over 18 and have read the usage instructions before diving right in.** The type of blade you choose will govern your cutting technique. I use a Swann Morton number 11 blade and Swann Morton ACM barrel number 1, as it is perfect for accurate cutting and getting into fiddly corners. You can buy them in craft shops, or via my online shop (www.paperpandacuts.co.uk). Keep a good supply of disposable blades, as they quickly become blunt and must be changed regularly. For many people, a round **barrel handle** is more comfortable to use than the usual flat handle that is often supplied. Dispose of used blades safely using a **blade remover unit** – a plastic box that removes and stores blades without you having to touch them.

A rubber **self-healing cutting mat** prevents your scalpel from slipping and cutting your hands, and also protects your worktop or table. Cutting mats come in different sizes and many of them have a useful ruled grid.

Tracing paper is useful for transferring your image to a piece of paper.

A sharp **pencil** is essential for copying templates and also for tracing.

Experiment with different weights of **art paper** to find out which suits you best. (Avoid regular printer paper, which is terrible to cut and blunts your blade quickly.) In the UK and Europe, paper weight is measured in grams per square metre (gsm). In North America, it is done by weight (pounds) per ream. As a general rule, 150gsm paper (approx. US 220lbs per ream) is a good thickness for papercutting use. Most office paper is thinner – around 70–80gsm (approx. US 100lbs per ream). I recommend Canford 150gsm (US 220lbs per ream) in ivory for the main body of the papercuts – they also have a large range of coloured paper for decorative infills.

Use a **metal ruler** to cut straight edges, as a scalpel will cut into plastic or wooden rulers.

A **set of compasses** is useful for making tiny holes in the paper – eye holes, for example.

A **glue stick** is used to stick designs to backing paper, or to stick coloured paper to sections of your design. If you want to raise the paper off the surface slightly to achieve a three-dimensional effect, use adhesive **foam pads** or **glue dots**.

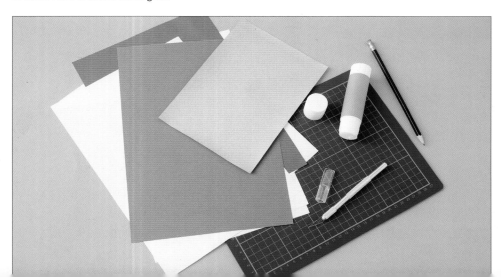

Techniques

The templates in this book have been made from real papercuts at actual size. If you are a beginner, you could enlarge them slightly on a photocopier, or scan them and enlarge them using your printer settings or design software. However, as long as you have a sharp blade and a bit of practice under your belt, it is fine just to trace them and cut at the sizes shown here.

Practise cutting some basic shapes first on a plain piece of paper and see how much pressure you need to apply to get a clean cut. If your blade is new, then you should not need to press very hard. This can result in hand cramps, snapped blades and an inability to control the scalpel – no fun at all. Take regular breaks, preferably involving tea and cake!

Instructions for each project:

1 Photocopy or scan and print the template onto your chosen paper. Printers tend to copy easily onto weights of paper up to about 150gsm (approx. US 220lbs per ream). Alternatively, trace the image from the book onto paper for cutting.

2 Start cutting the most difficult section of a design first, or the parts that you do not feel confident cutting – this ensures that if you make a mistake you have not wasted much time.

3 Take your time, change your blade every 10–15 minutes and take regular breaks to give your hand and neck a rest. A sloped surface such as a tilted drawing board is an advantage.

4 Do not worry about rubbing out pencil marks on the back of the paper, as they will not be seen and erasing may damage the paper. You will be working on the reverse of the cut.

5 Resist the temptation to remove the excess paper as you go along. Keeping it in place helps to stabilise the design and you are also less likely to snag the design on your sleeve/jewellery/cat. When complete, cut away the excess paper rather than pushing the design out with your finger, as this will stop it from ripping and you can see if any parts need to be re-cut.

Apple Tree

Materials:

Tracing paper

Pencil

Ivory paper

Glitter paper
   and glue stick
   (optional)

Tools:

Scalpel (barrel handle
   and spare blades)

Self-healing cutting mat

Container for
   blade disposal

Tip: Frame the large apple tree and give it as a gift to a special friend. Place red sparkly glitter paper behind the hearts in the tiny apples, or thread them with ribbon and hang them as decorations.

This special apple tree would make a lovely gift for a child's teacher. Display it where the light can come through.

Beautiful Bookmarks

Materials:

Tracing paper

Pencil

Ivory paper

Coloured paper

Glitter paper

Glue stick

Tools:

Scalpel (barrel handle and spare blades)

Self-healing cutting mat

Container for blade disposal

Tip: Place some sparkly glitter paper behind the largest heart shape. Back both of these bookmarks with a darker colour, gluing them at the top for a double-layer effect. You could also laminate them for durability.

These bookmarks make great gifts for all sorts of occasions. Try the hearts for a Valentine gift, and the tree bookmark as a birthday gift.

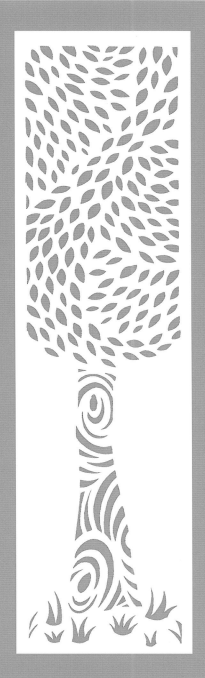

Butterfly

Materials:

Tracing paper
Pencil
Ivory paper
Coloured paper
Glitter paper
Glue stick

Clear film in various
  colours (optional)

Tools:

Scalpel (barrel handle and
  spare blades)
Self-healing cutting mat
Container for blade disposal

Tip: Try backing some sections of the butterfly with different colours of clear film instead of the coloured paper and hang from a window for a stained glass effect.

The butterfly is a positive symbol the world over. This design lends itself to the addition of lots of colour.

Coffee Pot

Materials:

Tracing paper
Pencil
Ivory paper

Tools:

Scalpel (barrel handle
   and spare blades)
Self-healing cutting mat
Container for
   blade disposal

Tip: Try placing some coloured paper behind the flowers to add an extra splash of colour.

Pep up your kitchen with this steaming coffee pot, complete with cheeky perching bird.

Pretty Place Cards

Materials:

Tracing paper

Pencil

Ivory paper

Tools:

Scalpel (barrel handle and spare blades)

Self-healing cutting mat

Container for blade disposal

Tip: Do not cut all the way to the edge of these place cards. Notice that the purple cutting guidelines on the template stop short of either edge – this is where you fold, rather than cut.

These place cards are too good to write on. Try using removable adhesive stickers so that they can be reused.

Quill Pen

Materials:

Tracing paper

Pencil

Paper

Red glitter paper
and glue stick
(optional)

Tools:

Scalpel (barrel handle
and spare blades)

Self-healing cutting mat

Container for
blade disposal

Tip: Cut the 'ink' lines first using a fresh blade.
Place a little piece of red glitter paper behind
the tiny heart for a subtle accent.

*This makes a lovely decoration
for a home office – mount it on
coloured card for extra impact.*

Bouquet

Materials:

Tracing paper
Pencil
Ivory paper
Coloured paper
Adhesive dots

Tools:

Scalpel (barrel handle
and spare blades)
Self-healing cutting mat
Container for
blade disposal

Tip: Place coloured paper behind the veined leaves and the central petals, and use adhesive pads or dots to raise the papercut slightly from the backing.

Flowers are so versatile that this bouquet is perfect for a greeting card or picture frame.

Owl Always Love You

Materials:
Tracing paper
Pencil
Ivory paper

Tools:
Scalpel (barrel handle
and spare blades)
Self-healing cutting mat
Container for
blade disposal

Tip: Use a fresh blade to cut the star 'strings' first, as they are probably the trickiest part of this design.

This design makes a lovely card for a night owl – or someone whose baby keeps them up at night!

Love Hearts

Materials:

Tracing paper
Pencil
Ivory paper
Twine (optional)

Tools:

Scalpel (barrel handle
  and spare blades)
Self-healing cutting mat
Container for
  blade disposal

Tip: The smaller hearts have little holes for you to thread them with twine and hang them as decorations. You could even attach them to the large heart and hang as a mobile.

This love heart is perfect for a Valentine card – simply mount on coloured card and write your own message.

Mermaid

Materials:

Tracing paper

Pencil

Ivory paper

Iridescent paper
and glue stick
(optional)

Tools:

Scalpel (barrel handle
and spare blades)

Self-healing cutting mat

Container for
blade disposal

Tip: Placing some iridescent paper behind the
tail will give the mermaid an extra sparkle.

*Mount this mermaid on sea-green
or blue card as a pretty bathroom
decoration, or make a birthday card
for your own little mermaid!*

Floral Picture Frame

Materials:

Tracing paper
Pencil
Ivory paper
Coloured paper
Glue stick

Tools:

Scalpel (barrel handle
    and spare blades)
Self-healing cutting mat
Container for
    blade disposal

Tip: Practise cutting straight lines before starting this design. If in doubt, leave them complete and just cut the floral parts – your picture frame will still look fabulous.

Frame your loved ones in this delicate design to show them off at their best.

Peacock

Materials:

Tracing paper
Pencil
Ivory paper
Coloured paper
Glue stick
Iridescent paper
(optional)

Tools:

Scalpel (barrel handle
and spare blades)
Self-healing cutting mat
Container for
blade disposal

Tip: You could use iridescent green and blue paper to accent some of the peacock's feathers before framing.

Proud as a peacock – this design deserves to be displayed in a prominent spot.

Fairy Glade

Materials:

Tracing paper
Pencil
Ivory paper
Coloured paper
Glue stick

Tools:

Scalpel (barrel handle
  and spare blades)
Self-healing cutting mat
Container for
  blade disposal

Tip: Keep your blade sharp for all the swirls and turn the page as you are cutting round them. Test cutting the eyelashes a few times with some spare paper and a fresh blade before attempting the final piece.

Cut this design as a card for a little girl's birthday, or a framed picture for her room.

32

Rainy Day

Materials:

Tracing paper

Pencil

Ivory paper

Coloured paper

Glue stick

Tools:

Scalpel (barrel handle
and spare blades)

Self-healing cutting mat

Container for
blade disposal

Tip: A rainbow-coloured umbrella will brighten anyone's day. Use pastels or primary colours and tiny dabs of glue on the edge of your knife to apply to the spines of the umbrella – this will help to stick the coloured paper in place.

You can personalise this cheery papercut with your choice of colour for the backing paper and the girl's umbrella.

Little Red Riding Hood

Materials:

Tracing paper
Pencil
Ivory paper

Tools:

Scalpel (barrel handle
and spare blades)
Self-healing cutting mat
Container for
blade disposal

Tip: For a different effect, cut this design from dark paper and frame it using an old book page as the backing paper – especially if you can find an old (and no longer readable) copy of the original story. Alternatively, you could write your own story, type it up on an old typewriter for an interesting effect, or print it on recycled paper.

This fairytale papercut is perfect as a framed picture for a child's playroom.

Woodland Friends

Materials:

Tracing paper

Pencil

Ivory paper

Tools:

Scalpel (barrel handle
    and spare blades)

Self-healing cutting mat

Container for
    blade disposal

Set of compasses
    (for eye holes)

Tip: Cut the skipping rope first using a fresh blade, as this is the most difficult part. Use a set of compasses to make eyes for the characters. Ensure you push the point through from the front to the back, as this prevents the paper protruding from the front of the finished cut.

These happy woodland friends create a great papercut to stick to a door or window as a welcome sign.

Snowy Day

Materials:

Tracing paper
Pencil
Ivory paper
Coloured paper
Glue stick

Tools:

Scalpel (barrel handle
and spare blades)
Self-healing cutting mat
Container for
blade disposal

Tip: Nobody said snowflakes had to be completely round! Have fun with this one – it does not have to be perfectly cut to look effective. You can frame your cut or display it using small pegs on twine.

This festive snow scene is perfect as a Christmas card – add a little sparkle to the door and windows with some glitter paper.

Cute Gift Tags

Materials:

Tracing paper
Pencil
Ivory paper
Coloured paper
Glue stick
Ribbon (optional)

Tools:

Scalpel (barrel handle and spare blades)
Self-healing cutting mat
Container for blade disposal
Set of compasses (for eye holes)

Tip: Back these tags with dark paper of the same shape, cutting the hole in the same place, and tie them together with ribbon for a double-layer effect.

These gift tags add a personal note to a present for someone special.

Christmas Tree

Materials:

Tracing paper

Pencil

Ivory paper

Coloured paper

Glitter

Glue stick

Tools:

Scalpel (barrel handle and spare blades)

Self-healing cutting mat

Container for blade disposal

Tip: Go crazy and fill the bauble circles with different colours. Do not forget the glitter!

Use this festive tree as a card, or attach a string to the star to make a hanging decoration.

Unicorn

Materials:

Tracing paper

Pencil

Ivory paper

Coloured paper

Glue stick

Glitter paper
    (optional)

Tools:

Scalpel (barrel handle
    and spare blades)

Self-healing cutting mat

Container for
    blade disposal

Tip: A touch of glitter will make this unicorn extra special. Place different colours of glitter paper behind each heart along the centre of the body for a sparkly effect.

This highly decorative papercut, using the ancient symbol of the unicorn, will appeal to everyone.

Publisher's Note

You are invited to visit the author's website:

www.paperpandacuts.co.uk